Anonymous

America

A Dramatic Poem

Anonymous

America
A Dramatic Poem

ISBN/EAN: 9783337336899

Printed in Europe, USA, Canada, Australia, Japan

Cover: Foto ©Thomas Meinert / pixelio.de

More available books at **www.hansebooks.com**

AMERICA

A DRAMATIC POEM.

NEW-YORK:
ANSON D. F. RANDOLPH,
683 BROADWAY.
1863.

PREFACE.

This little poem was chiefly written in the beginning of the year 1862, and reflects events and feelings more peculiarly belonging to that epoch of the terrible and momentous struggle which still convulses our land. But though its particular form may retain the impress of that moment, yet it is hoped that it will not on that account be found destitute of power to recall the magnitude of the issue, the awful solemnity of the crisis.

Some allusion is made to the unfriendly attitude of Europe. While, however, we dwell sadly on the disappointment occasioned by encountering a spirit of hostility, where the most opposite sentiment had been anticipated, let us still remember that the heart of humanity every where beats with us whether consciously or not.

In this faith let us strengthen ourselves. And let us recall with gratitude the names of some even beyond the ocean, who have not hesitated to speak for us in this our time of trouble; above all, that of Count Gasparin, who, with such unwearied patience, such earnestness of affection, has studied into the spirit of our history and national life, and following us in every step of this painful struggle, has plead our cause so nobly and so faithfully before the tribunal of public opinion in Europe.

May the hope and expectation of such friends meet with no disappointment through our unworthiness of the part we are called to play in the destinies of mankind.

AMERICA.

Mountains of Virginia—Night—Genius of America—Alone.

AMERICA.

Weep! weep! my clouds, drench the dull night
    with tears,
Ye winds of heaven, from every quarter come
Shriek forth my pain, and with your outcry wild
Let thunders mix their voice: let all the hills
Ashamed of dumbness, send some echo back
Responsive to my grief. — But though ye poured
Your fountains dry, O heavens! though ye should
    rage,
Ye thunders, till no sound were left to shake
The groaning sphere, yet would ye suit no more
Than summer dews, or birds that sing at dawn,

To speak the measures of mine agony.
Well dost thou sit, O darkness! on these hills,
Well dost thou clothe about with robe obscure
The soil once glorious, now with shame defiled,
Disowned of all her heroes, and by doom,
Just as the nod of heaven, condemned to drink
The poisoned cup that to the mother's lips
The daughter's hand upheld. — Lo! in mine ears
The battle sounds afar. I hear the shock
Of arms, the deadly clash of meeting foes.
The hoofs of war tear up the sacred sod
That bore the common sires. The bullet flies
By brother aimed at brother. They that fed
As one upon my breast, each to this heart
Dear as the inmost currents of its life,
Wrestle together in the mad embrace
Not loosed till death for one or both divide
The firm-strung sinewy strength, with palsying
    hand
Smite down a crown of manhood in the dust.

AMERICA.

O heavens! O earth! look on, and see what
    grief
Provokes my bitter outcry! — unto mine
Compare not yours, O mothers that do sit
Gazing, with eyes that can not see for tears,
On faces of dead offspring, — not with yours
I count my sorrows, — but if one there be,
One miserable mother in the land
Against whose life the nursling of her love
Hath lifted murderous hand, — against the life
That was its source and fount, hath lifted up
The thrice accursed parricidal stroke,
Then let her come, for she hath known my woe,
Then let her sit and mix her tears with mine.
— Yet she, mayhap, would be some mother stern,
Some cruel stepdame, and no tender care
Had taught more reverence, — but a thorny bed
Her bosom proved, nor could they learn so late
A better lore, who from her lips had heard
No word of pity drop, no lesson mild

Swaying to tempers sweet their tender age.
But such unto my favorite sons was I?
Who whispered—who—the fierce and dreadful doubt
That so it had been better—that less love
Had wrought less hate?—What fiend now shakes
    my soul
Accusing weak indulgence of this fruit
Bitter to taste as ashes of the grave?
  Ah! woe is me! my children, woe is me!
Before whose eyes is set from day to day
This piteous sight, than which I think the earth
Hath none more piteous, where of those who
    formed
One prosperous household, one fraternal band,
Part stand around the mother to defend
With sword and blood, part spurred with impious
    rage
Press on to take her life. Woe! woe! is me,
Who brings me comfort? O ye winds of night!
Ye that have searched earth's utmost corners out,

And spoiled them of their secrets, let some word
Fall with sweet healing on my burning wound!

VOICE OF THE SOUTH WIND.

What wilt thou have, O melancholy one!
What wilt thou learn of me?

AMERICA.

Sweet is thy voice,
Sweet in mine ears, O South!

SOUTH WIND.

No happy word
Is set unto its music.

AMERICA.

Say not so.
Thou on whose dewy wings is lingering still
The scented breath of gardens far away
That never cease to bloom, but month by month
The rose unfolds her heart, and woos the sun
To hide amid her robes more splendid rays

Of crimson or of gold. Methinks I hear
Beneath thy sigh, the rustling sound that creeps
Among the tall magnolias, that reflect
From burnished leaves, like shields, the moon's pale
gleam.
I hear the myriad voices that ascend
From pathless forests, silent all the day,
But when the night his sudden mantle flings,
Begins tumultuous revel,—nature's joy
Unchecked, exultant, and until the dawn
The wild vociferous uproar doth not cease.

SOUTH WIND.

So, could I heal thee!

AMERICA.

Through the dull lagoons
I hear the waters, sobbing as they go,
And from the sand-bound coasts whose whitening
line

AMERICA.

Wearies from day to day the straining sight
Of lookers, out at sea, mine ear there greets
An echo, as of thunder, where his rage
The vexed Atlantic pours, and seeks to draw
Back to his yesty deep the groaning shores,
Where yet his restless fury heaps amain
The spoil of deep sea-bottoms, and builds out
The habitable land with increase got
Out of the bosom of his hungry wave.

SOUTH WIND.

How like wind-harassed waves, the stormy sighs
Chase one another through thy laboring breath!

AMERICA.

Methinks I see the broad and whitening fields,
Dumb in the starlight, ripe, but not for food,
Snowy, but not with cold. Betwixt their rows
Shall busy feet be moving, on the morn,
And sable hands be thrust in contrast strange

Amid the stainless fruit, to gather in
The harvest pure, whereof the world is glad.

SOUTH WIND.

Alas! for this the world shall ne'er be glad.

AMERICA.

O vexing wind! the voices of my sons,
My well-beloved! I hear amid thy sighs.
My fair and noble sons, on whom have fallen
All bounties of my love, the chosen gifts
Of earth and heaven — I hear, but not discern
The pleasant sounds. Interpret thou for me.

SOUTH WIND.

Thou hearest, O thou mother sad! too well.

AMERICA.

My proud and beauteous race, for whom I bore
A thousand sorrows, whom to spare one fear

AMERICA.

I gave my strength, my glory, and my hope,
Yea, but to shield them when their summer blood
Welled up within them as a fount defiled
Of tyrannous design, and purpose fixed
On wild and barbarous use of savage right;
Lent them, while all the world looked on and
    frowned,
The bright and stainless honor of my name,
To shield them from their shame, nor gave one
    thought
That so on me its blackening guilt must fall,
To be washed out in blood—their blood and mine.
Tell me not now, thou false, deceitful breath,
All are against me, all; that not one voice
Is raised to plead in presence of the rest
The dear and filial claim, to noble souls
Sacred forever, last to lose its hold
On those most reckless of all law beside,
That not one heart beats quicker, when some word
Stirs the old memories of those happier days,

When, from our seat, in union and in pride,
We scoffed at danger and defied the world.

SOUTH WIND.

Not one! Not one!

AMERICA.

Thou art too deaf to hear.
How canst thou know what thoughts in silence
    brood
Where fear is master, and the uttered word
Were like a solemn sentence, bearing death
Home to the speaker's heart, e'er yet his lips
Had ceased their motion? Many now do wait,
Faithful in voiceless patience, many more
To dull despair have yielded up the truth
That yet is mine, though hope be stifled long
Beneath the weight of grief. Ah! me, ah! me,
My heart is racked with anguish, and anew
My wounds are felt to bleed. — Ill-omened voice

AMERICA.

I'll no more of thee; from the East there comes
A cooler breath; unto my burning brow
It brings a freshening moisture from the deep;
Unto my heart, some message good and pure,
Conferring strength, and bracing up to deed
Heroic, urging on the fainting soul
To hope, to nobler zeal, to victory.
Some message from the shores beyond the sea,
From sisters well beloved, and honored well,
Who, having known in part what grief I bear,
Put forth a hand, or, if not so, a voice
To cheer me, that not utterly I fail.
Answer! swift messenger of rising suns,
What happy omens of a coming morn
Their loving eyes have seen, who watch for me
All through this murky night, in watch-towers set
Of ancient days in heights beyond the clouds.

VOICE OF THE EAST WIND.

No happy omen do their eyes discern

Whose eager looks another way are bent
Than where the dawn, if such remain for thee,
Shall lift the dusky edges of thy night;
Whose glances drink the blackness of thy shame
With more delight than ever fairest rays
Of crowned Auroras in the flaming east.

AMERICA.

What is this word, what is this note of ill?
Prithee shrill blast, blow shriller, that mine ear
May not mistake thine import.

EAST WIND.

Dost thou mark
How flies the shout of triumph still, as flies
Across your billowy waste some fresher tale
Of sorrow that hath met thee, some new stroke
That bows thy head to earth?

AMERICA.

I hear, I hear

AMERICA. 17

Strange sounds of exultation, what they mean
I know not.

EAST WIND.

Flatter! flatter not thine heart,
Helpless art thou, and hopeless, if thy help
Or hope from other than thyself must come.
Alone thou standest in thy bitter need,
Alone and friendless. Scoffed at by the world,
By saints unpitied, for thy sin that brought
This evil on thee, and by sinners scorned
For that thy pride had lifted thee too high
For brooking of their own, and now, that fallen,
The sweetness of revenge, without the cost,
Rewards the long impatience of their wish.

AMERICA.

Tell me of her, the noble one that sits
Alone amid the seas, her from whose breast
I drew my heart's best life, whose tongue is mine,
Whose glories are my glories, whom to owe

All that has lifted me above the rest,—
Save that I dared to claim my separate right,
And claiming hold it — is my willing boast.
Tell me that word which now to all the rest
She adds at such an hour, when peril hangs
So deadly, threatening all to both most dear,
Tell me the word in that beloved tongue
Whose accents yet shall ring, clear, bold, and
    sweet,
The world around, and all its sleepers wake.
So her own lark at morn, up springs and leaves
The misty ground, and soars and sings so loud,
Up! up! for now the sun has left his bed,
No time for dreams and dewy slumbers more,
Up! up! with me, to meet the golden morn.

EAST WIND.

Alas! alas!

AMERICA.

Hast thou no more reply?

AMERICA. 19

England is of her many conquests sure,
Who, in the girdle of her rule, includes
The habitable earth, and makes the sea
Her highway. England sits with blindfold eyes,
Like justice, and the even balance holds
Which, who by bold rebellious act dares move
Straight downward goes and settles his own doom.
Happy! thrice happy land, of all I know!
Who, in the dear affection of her sons,
Makes chiefest boast, nor shall she ever blush
To name her noble offspring, stout and brave:
For her they count no drop of blood too dear,
And she their love with equal love repays.
Yet has she tasted sorrow, so can know
Part that I prove, and from her happy lot
By contrast guess the rest.

EAST WIND.
But not to mourn,

Rather with hideous mockery to deride
Of rude and tuneless laughter.

AMERICA.

It is well!
But there was yet another, one whose hand
Placed firm on mine when there was bitter need,
Once nerved me for my conflict. She whose step
Once in this race was foremost,—from whose lips
Went forth that clarion note of "Liberty,
Equality, and Brotherhood," for man.
It sounded far, its echoes have not died,
Not even to her own hearing, though she close
Reluctant ears, for still it shall return
Thrown back in myriad voices from all shores
That men inhabit, till the time shall come,
That she hath learnt once more to sing and shout,
And join with clearer notes that chorus sweet,
Knowing the meaning now, which once unknown
And from her thought far absent, when her call

Was loudest, was not claimed at such demand.
Then in its stead came horror, blood, and death,
Reason's unthroning; then old tyrannies
Bound on with bands of iron, forged anew
In that fierce fire of horror; then a seal
Set on despair for many weary days
Wherein the light is hidden, though the sun
Lives still amid the heavens. Tell me of her,
Though scarce I hope, for those are passed away
Whose names are in my heart, when with my tongue
I utter hers.

EAST WIND.

Why shouldst thou further ask,
Since none stand with thee?

AMERICA.

Yea! for of them all
These two, the first and noblest, lead alone
The van of nations. Silence, O my heart!

Silence! keep down my tears. I shall not weep,
Nor fail, but gather up my single might,
And dare the hour alone. Once, once I stood
In joy upon my solitary shore.
Fearless I stood, nor did I seek their love,
Strong in the might within me, strong in these,
These household traitors, then I called aloud
The world was silent listening for the voice
That signalled joy and hope to all the race.

EAST WIND.

Now to thyself returns thy boastful shout
In drear reverberations. Lo! the fruit
Of all thy sowing, while the seed is known
In this rank poisonous crop, that kills the air
And with its exhalations foul defiles
The very heavens.

AMERICA.

Mock on! mock on! 'tis meet

AMERICA.

That scorn be joined to sorrow, and my heart
By one more stroke be proved, that men may
   know
What stuff 'tis made of, whether this, or that,
Shall force it to its breaking; yet I think
There's something in it yet that shall survive
A longer crushing. Though the weight of years,
Packed full of grief, should hinder every throb,
And make it beat in time with funeral bells
That toll the sleeper's way, when loving friends
Bear him to his low chamber in the dust;
Yea! though 'twere buried, buried in a grave
As deep as to the mountain's steadfast roots,
And with the mountains hurled like monuments
To mark its hope as ended; yet I think
'Twould beat beneath them still, and on a day,
In one great act upgathering all the force
Matured in silence, startle dreamers round
With throes of resurrection. In my soul
I hear the whisper of a secret voice,

The prophecy of life. No hand profane
Shall quench in utter night that fire divine,
Which for the world's deliverance in me burns.

EAST WIND.

Strange hope thou utterest, and a bolder scope
Hast set unto thy thoughts than suits the bounds
And destinies of nations.

AMERICA.

I will speak
Of former things, and will recall the days
Of youth, now far behind me, by a gap
As wide as death, cut off from that which is.
When thus I stood, and cried with voice as clear
As bugles, or as trumpets, that cheer on
To victory; Lo! I wait, I wait to know,
Ye lands, the high decrees of destiny.
The glorious offspring I of all your strength
And heir of all your greatness, yea than all

AMERICA.

More nobly portioned, where I stand alone
Betwixt these oceans, whose wide rolling waves
Are servitors to me, to bring me spoils
Of many isles; whereon I well shall feed
With inward wealth, unsummed and measureless.
Rich in all bounties I, of generous heaven,
And earth beneath, and of the flowing deep,
But most in hope, that to your wearied age
But faintly comes. All hail! ye golden years,
All hail! thou wondrous future that is mine,
Since light is yours, and wisdom without end,
Prosperity and joy. Through all my veins
The bounding pulses play, my heart is set,
My eye is fixed on summits yet unclimbed,
Blue in the misty distance, shining fair
In all soft glories of the morning sun.
There, there await my eager, panting steps,
The unknown splendors of the great "to be."
Farewell! farewell! old champions in this race,
Your time is passed. O sisters! ye did well,

But now your time is passed. Here where I stand
Bounteous and full, I call, I shout aloud,
My voice to earth's remotest bound goes forth;
Ho! all ye poor, who have no food nor rest,
Ye to whom life is bitter, ye for whom
There seems on earth no room. Lo! here is room,
Food, freedom, rest. See how they leave your arms,
Your unfed children, with their hunger weak,
Your persecuted wanderers — they to me
Come flying in their need, and I for all
Have ready welcome and a full supply.
I who have broken for myself the yoke
That once your tyrants forced my neck to bear,
Have such a heart as beats in sympathy
With all that suffer wrong, and loves the slave,
(Save that upon one neck I place my foot
And hold it firm, wherein my will or right

AMERICA.

Let no man question,) therefore, when ye see
My starry banner floating to the wind
Rejoice ye lands, and shout for liberty.

VOICE OF THE NORTH WIND.

Lo! I, the rapid messenger of storms,
With face set Southward, whose wide whirling
 wings
Shake down amid their motion flights of rain,
Cold dews of night, sharp frosts, and mantling
 snows,
And with a touch, in many a torpid brain
Quicken the stagnant life, and set in flow
The sluggish blood in many a drooping heart.
I bid thee hail, O glorious hope of men!
And bring thee loyal greetings, love, and faith,
From sons that fly to aid, with weaponed arm,
And lavished blood, and treasure without stint,
The mother's desperate need.

AMERICA.

Sons against sons,
My sweetest tidings.

NORTH WIND.

Who shall dare to weigh
Claims filial and fraternal? who shall see
The brother's hand, if in its frenzied grasp
Glistens the accursed blade of parricides?
These ponder not in unresolved despair
The question's awful terms, but seeing clear,
Through all dim clouds of horror, fear, and doubt,
The one solution, push aside with scorn
Revolting thoughts, and make their shuddering
   wills
Leap forward to that fixed and holy work,
Sole hope and sole deliverance.

AMERICA.

Is it so?

AMERICA.

O fate! not yet, not yet my heart accepts
Thy hard decree, but like a stormy deep,
Lashing its rocky barriers, so my soul
Spends its own strength in wild and fierce dissent,
Not breaks nor alters thine.

NORTH WIND.

      What further word
Of mine can bring thee comfort?

AMERICA.

      Yet speak on.
For what if all were traitors? Though in part
The house be fallen, yet that some pillars stand
To hold the whole from ruin — it is well.

NORTH WIND.

Faint is thy voice, and joyless, yet not faint
Their hearts who love thee. All thy mighty
  North

Moves as a single man, swayed by one thought,
Led by one counsel, to retrieve thy doom,
Even though at cost of all. Who treasured once
Their hard-earned gold, now cast it down, with
    scorn
Uncounted, in thy service; who loved life,
Love it the more, that they may sell it dear,
Offering the price to thee. Here lovers miss
The eyes that were their morning, brothers press
A last dear kiss on sisters' cheeks, and sons
Turn not again at hearing that God-speed
From mothers' lips, that falter not though pale;
No doubt nor murmur's heard, only each one
Asks his own heart the question, "What have I?"
How shall my little strength be made to serve
The moment's solemn uses? So thy thought
Controls all motions, sways with force supreme
Each warm heart's leaping impulse, guides and
    thrills
Fingers, that over slender to uplift

The heavy sword that must undo thy wrong,
Are all the fitter for a meeker toil,
That helps thy helpers, comforts those who give
Their manhood and their all, to comfort thee.
And be not hopeless, for where faith is found
Strength also dwells, and fullness. Turn and look;
Know thy true-hearted North, her step is firm
Though light and buoyant, through the tide of
    youth
That swells her veins, the measure of glad hope
That in her heart she bears. Her brow is clear,
Open as heaven, with majesty there writ
Of purpose measured still with love and truth,
And in her gentle eyes the steady fire
Burns tender, deep, and true. Oh! trust her well,
While with slow aim, deliberate, one by one
Her giant blows descend to cut thy way
Straight on to victory, while that loyal faith,
Like leaven, shall work from hers to hearts less
    firm,

Her courage high inspire the feebler breasts,
Till with the subtle force that ever lives
In noble deeds, she win the recreants back,
And former days return, to crown thy brows
With more than former glories.

AMERICA.

Can it be?
Yet less than this were nothing.—For their hearts
That hate me, for these only do I pine;
No other victory, other were defeat.
How can I make my children to my slaves?

NORTH WIND.

Yet force must be first winner, strike the sword,
Whose sight still maddens, from the mad one's
    grasp,
Release some true hearts from the spell of fear;
Some that of truth or treachery make a badge
According to the fashion, giving leave

That to unpin and this to fasten on
A sleeve that matches either.

    AMERICA.

     Heaven speed
My champions, for their own cause, and for mine,
And for my lost ones.

    NORTH WIND.

      Hear the tramp of feet
That breaks the night. Her gathering thousands
  march,
Their horses' hoofs make music on the ground
That shakes beneath them. In the midst is heard
The rumbling of her dread artillery,
Whose flaming mouths e'er long shall hold dis-
  course
Than reason's self more potent, while on high
Above the whole, its sign and argument,
That banner floats, out of whose starry heaven

No missing orb is dropped, but perfect still
Its constellations shine, and with the past
Link on a glorious future.

AMERICA.

      Yet, on these
I did not pour my favors. They it seems
Are prosperous,— feel within their honest hearts
The swelling, grateful tide, whose wealth must pour
About my feet, as author of their good.
And yet methinks, 'twas but a meagre choice
I left these brave ones, when my best was set
At service of my darlings. Rough the ways
I taught their feet to walk in from the first,
And on a hard, scarce cultivable soil,
Bade them with sweat of brow, and calloused hands,
Exact therefrom their portion. Rude the storms
That vexed their coasts, or through their valleys bleak

Swept chill and void of pity, while the snows
Covered for many months their scanty fields,
And summer's proper measure ever lacked
When longest. If they found upon my thorn
Some flowers, I knew it not, and if the flower
Into such fruit has ripened as I see,
Let them their own good hearts and steadfast wills,
Their days and nights of cheerful labor thank,
And leave to me my wisdom and my choice,
To smell my rose, — my rose, that dropping now
Its petals one by one, leaves me to feel
On torn and bleeding lips, what stays behind,
That sweet show perished, and that fragrance fled.

NORTH WIND.

They will not hear thee, but with shouts and joy,
And loyal love, and numbering one by one
The blessings got through thee, repeat thy name,
Calling on all to know, and to confess

No bands of duty and of faith so strong
As those which unto thee thy children bind.
Nor will they hear dispraised that sterner lot,
Whose helpful hardness braced their sinews up
To manlier vigor — braced their minds within
To choose from day to day the nobler part,
And by the needful discipline of pain
Taught to discern 'twixt pleasures false and true,
'Twixt boasts of present power, and that whose
    base
Eternal, shall not shake; 'twixt license wild,
Or willful mastery, and the glorious use
Of freedom, whereunto the soul is born.

AMERICA.

Yet have I robbed them, with unwilling eyes
Beheld their growing wealth, and saw them claim
The larger place in counsel. Soon, I said,
These will stand foremost to uphold my name
In sight of men; their choice too much prevail,

Changing a thousand customs, dear through use,
Whether for worse or better. Fool! to see
So far, and not what now I see too well
Too late, what black and infamous abyss
Already yawned to swallow all my pride,
Unless these loving hands prove strong enough
To hold me up from ruin. So I mocked,
Reproved, and checked them, ever more pushed back
Their forward steps, but still within the code
Of that most perfect, just, and balanced law
That over me and them I set at first
Our safeguard, and our warranty of good.
That bound I never passed, nor these approached
Its sacred limits, but with holy awe
Inviolate held what they the bulwark deemed
Of human liberties and natural right.
But those have laughed at love alike, and fear,
Me, and my highest gift at once they spurn,
And by one bold, high-handed act of crime,

With treachery for its warrant, will undo
The whole world's history, turn the ages back
On their slow march, to find again that night,
Whence in slow pain, at price of toil and blood,
Earth's heroes had released them, scorning life,
For happier men to purchase better days.

VOICE OF THE WEST WIND.

I bear thee from thy children of the West
Victorious greetings, and outrun with news
Their loyal feet, who haste to crown thy brows
With earliest laurels of this fateful strife.

AMERICA.

What word hast thou?

WEST WIND.

   Forth from their prairies rushed
The gallant bands, soon as the tidings came
Of laws reviled, and fealty despised,

And danger threatening through a treacherous blow
All that uplifts with thee thy faithful sons
Above the common lot. With valiant hands,
Armed or unarmed they came, with hearts on fire,
And brave intent to rescue or to die.
So furnished, swept they down upon thy foes,
And from Virginia's western quarter first
Banished the fell invader, drove him well
Within his rebel bounds. On flying feet
Of consternation, strewing as he went
Arms, baggage, tents, and furniture of war,
He shunned the furious onset, and defeat
Still marked from field to field his way in blood.
Now from his lair beyond the ridgy hills
With greedy disappointment still he eyes
The rescued booty, and but waits the hour,
To spring again, and seize on all he's lost.
While faithful still the saviours of the soil
Stand watching to defend, and from his rear
He yet may hear a shout more terrible

Than first dismayed him, then with vain attempt
Strive to elude his captors, but their bands
Shall hold him fast, and lead him to thy feet.

AMERICA.

Glad news of sorrow! joy whose welcoming
Is bitter with my tears, — but not with mine
For many, counting life itself too cheap
To buy such tidings, hearing, with no smile
Reward the bringer, but, as David, cry,
My son! my son! my brother! would to God
That I had died for thee.

WEST WIND.

        Art so displeased?

AMERICA.

But black should be my triumph's livery,
And solemn funeral marches usher in
My pageant, when with spoils of victory

AMERICA.

I enter at the gates, this contest done.
Strange contest where the conqueror gains in loss,
The conquered lose to gain, and I their woes
Must weep, while they, by chastisement made wise,
Receive the forfeit love once more, and care
And privilege of sons.

WEST WIND.

      No welcome hast
For happy tidings?

AMERICA.

      Yet through all its pain
Doth not my heart leap up to hear these deeds
Of my last born, my warrior of the West?

WEST WIND.

Expect more glorious things, for now their foot
Stands planted where the giant waters meet,
That bear the commerce of their golden soil

Down to the Southern sea. Thence shall they
    hold
That mighty border, on whose shifting line
Rebellion's stormy waves now surge and lash,
Bidding the firm hills tremble. These shall make
Their hearts the barrier, and with strong advance
Drive the proud billows backward, till they meet
The nether sea, and in its depths be lost.

AMERICA.

Yet who assures me? Who discerns the end?
What sign rebukes my fear, or promised grace
Gives me an anchor through this night of storm,
A hold upon the heavens, which now no voice
Permit to hear, but such as smites my soul
With wrathful accents, and imports despair?
How shall I, gallant sons, cry, "Lift your hearts,
Courage!" "God speed ye well," while still re-
    turns,
As if my voices echo from all lands,

AMERICA.

The inauspicious cry, " 'Tis done, and fallen
The glory of thy greatness; know it well:
Being fallen, aspire no more, nor think to mend
With rivets new the broken chain that held
Thy destinies from shipwreck, or cement
A violated league, that was no more,
With vain expense of blood."

VOICE OF THE RIVERS.

Ah! me. Ah! me.
I wonder and cry out with thee,
  New and unthought agony
  Seizes on me suddenly,
  For of old my shining bands
  He laid upon the lands.
The net with skillful hands he wove,
  Beneath the sun its meshes shone,
  And in the pale-rayed moon;
  And every knot was set to prove
  Some mystery of love.

AMERICA.

Ah! me. Ah! me.
What hand hath rent, hath torn in twain,
Our cunning net, our shining chain?
Is the love of heaven in vain?
  That hath written its intent
  Over this fair continent;
Written plain in lines of light,
To be read by day or night?

Shall my waves then backward flow?
  Seek the sources whence they came,
In the mountains capped with snow,
  Or forgotten of their fame
  Slip into the gulf below?

VOICE OF THE MOUNTAINS.

Of an ancient race are we,
Barriers older than the soil,
Older than the sea.
Who shall break the strong decree,

By which He, the mighty One,
Lifted us to taste the sun?
Shall His word of power once more
Put an end to light and bliss,
Open up the drear abyss,
Where we dwelt with night before?
Shall we sleep with death again?
Since His signals speak in vain,
And the mortal nations know
Wall nor limit to their power,
Nor whither in their hour
Their rash usurping waves may flow?

VOICE OF THE SEAS.

I, Ocean, from the North, the East, the West,
  With forced retreat that day
Fled, at His stern behest,
  Who shaped her shores,
And broadly laid her bounds, with port and bay,

And harbors good, like mighty entrance doors
Set wide for commerce. One the line
  That from the northward swept
Down to the stormy gulf,
  Whose warmer waters leapt
With impulse strange, henceforth to meet,
With new embrace, by contrast sweet,
And by the voice divine,
My chilling tides, that roll
Ice laden from the pole;
And on her western shore,
With mighty surge and roar,
My billows broke in vain.
For He that said, "O land! be one."
  Made firmer his decree,
Than that strength-shattering waves of mine
Could foil the great design.
    One, therefore, let it be,
From North to South,
From rising unto setting sun.

AMERICA.

VOICE OF THE LAKES.

Midway the continent, behold!
    Our emerald waters dance,
    And, tipped with sunny gold,
Out of their lucid fountains glance
    To kiss the gladsome light.
So clear are we and bright,
E'er since His mighty hand
Pressed deep the fertile land,
And touched the living springs below.
In one unbroken chain
Half way from main to main,
Through basins wide, He bade them flow,
And said, "Bear up upon your breast,
O waves! the commerce of the West,
    And lead it to the sea.
Ye, on the North, for such a land
As now my wisest grace hath planned,
And closed about from strand to strand,
    A boundary shall be."

AMERICA.

Ah! me. Ah! me.
Still with his God at war, with nature still,
Is man, and ever thwarts with random spite
The will of sovereign love. Should I be vile
Even as he, and dare reproach that grace
Which, able to control, leaves free to choose
This creature frail, who still so awful power
Turns to his own destruction? I have heard
This always to be true, that God hath planned,
And man with scorn rejected, every good
That to his lot is suited. Eden first—
That lost, still some new garden, planted fair
With pleasant shoots thence rescued, all alike
His foot hath trampled, and the curse of thorns
Hath come upon it, through his wanton pride.
So, shall this last and fairest run to waste?
O destiny! O power of endless grace!
Forbid! forbid, the sacrilege, the shame,
The loss unsummed, that time shall not repair.

Give mercy, — now is time for grace, and proof
Of all-sufficient might — some way devise,
O wisdom! — sure a way is hid with thee,
A cure for all this madness of the heart,
And thou wilt heal. — But woe is me, I fear,
My spirit trembles in me, lest this time
God interpose not, since I know his plan
Gives little room for wonders; unto man,
Man's way he leaves, if he himself will slay,
No hand omnipotent shall strike aside
The dagger from its aim.

[Shades of Revolutionary heroes pass in solemn procession.

Ha! what new sight
Affrights the stars, and startles from their sleep
The shadow-cradling hills? — Sure to my thoughts
An answer, to mine unbelief a sign!
Or rather from my wild and teeming brain
A monstrous product, that to fancy's eyes
Appears than sense more real. . . .

O Shapes obscure!
That round the moonlit margin of the vale
Wind slow your ominous way, declare, speak out,
And with intelligible words make known
If such ye be, as unto me ye seem.

All's silence, — yet if ever from their graves
The dead upstarting, walk this world once more,
'Tis in such guise they come, and lo! the forms
And lineaments of heroes long asleep,
Known unto me each one — each one beloved.
With heads bowed low as if through weight of
    grief
'Twixt where I stand and yonder massive gloom
At solemn pace they glide, as if their ears
Heeded some spectral music, and anon
Each bends on me his melancholy gaze,
Then with a slow obeisance passes on.
O souls of patriots! could not death make strong
His fetters, but that ye must also come
To break my heart with memories?—Nay! put on

AMERICA.

The very robe of flesh ye wore of old,
Stand once more in your places, let men hear
Each voice severed, to those grand accents tuned,
That once compelled assent, though long withheld,
Even from the unwilling. It may be that then
The traitors will grow true, the faithless sons
Unto the fathers' creed return, the spoiled
And wasted heritage be fair once more
With pains of prosperous toil. Yet nay! yet nay!
Even so their blind eyes would refuse to see,
Their ears be deaf as ever. Since your graves,
Once hallowing all the soil, can not rebuke,
Nor former words remembered, all in vain
Your living lips would speak.

     Nay! who art thou?
O chief of heroes, and of patriots first!
Great father of thy country! proved thy tomb
Too narrow also, when its walls received
This tumult of our strife? Can trumpets break,
And shouts of war, and cannons with their roar,

So sacred peace? — Nay! turn not thou on me
The mild reproach that sits within thine eyes.
That can I not endure, for what in me
Of blame discernest? Clean I know my skirts,
But thy great work of life, undone! undone!
Except with mightier hand than ever yet,
God smite the evil, turn the torrent back
Of whelming wrath, as my avenger stand,
And take the victory.

    See! they pass, they pass,
The blackness of the night in yonder glen
Receives them — so they leave me to my woe.

CHORUS OF APOSTATE SPIRITS.

See! as if with sudden pain,
 Vanquished, to the earth she falls,
 Who the doubtful life recalls?
Let her lie there, ours the gain!

Who to me, of ancient time,
 Whispered warnings of a date,

AMERICA.

By the ordinance of fate
Set to misery and crime?

Not to-night, and not to-morrow,
Comes an end of human sorrow;
Mischief without us is brewing,
Man is still his own undoing.

Every gift that Heaven sends him
   Loses virtue as he takes it,
   With his sin a curse he makes it;
Nothing helps him, nothing mends him.

Therefore, I rejoice securely,
Holding now my throne more surely,
Knowing that no coming day
Holds for him a treasure, greater
Than his hand now flings away.

ANGEL OF COMFORT.

Hist! hist! she sleeps, — or is it rather death,

Or but a swoon of grief? Her languid lids
Betray no motion, on my hand no breath
Makes known she lives. O fair and noble head!
Art thou laid low forever? — is this end
Put to thy thoughts sublime, and the rude earth
So soon thy pillow? — yet it shall not be.
Rest, sleeper, on my heart, and if one spark
Of vital power yet linger, let this touch
Disturb its slumber,—let this kiss of mine,
Pressing thy two pale lips, send through thy veins
A kindling tide of warm and ruddy life,
And reënforce at once with full supplies
Its failing fount, to former health restored.

AMERICA.

Methought an evil presence hovered near
And bound my brows with iron.

ANGEL OF COMFORT.

None is here,
I only.

AMERICA.

What hast thou to do with me?

ANGEL OF COMFORT.

To bring thee comfort.

AMERICA.

Comfort?—even so
They mock the desperate!—yet I think thy look
Hath something in it that might cheer, though death
    Leered close behind thee. Prithee tell thy name.

ANGEL.

Even as mine office, is, for thee, my name.

AMERICA.

How wilt thou comfort such an one as I?

ANGEL.

Making thee turn thine eyes away from ill.

AMERICA.

Shall they then rest on naught?

ANGEL.

On good alone,
Until a little strengthened.

AMERICA.

Dost thou see
Good then? — that can not I.

ANGEL.

I bid thee look.

AMERICA.

I look on thee, and through so beauteous sight
My soul is fed with strength.

AMERICA.

ANGEL.

   I bid thee see
Cause of more hopeful courage.

AMERICA.

    Wilt thou name
Such cause more clearly?

ANGEL.

    Yet thou mayst prevail.

AMERICA.

Knowest thou that?—O sweet and tranquil voice!
Speak on.

ANGEL.

   What nation yet hath touched
Its pinnacle of greatness, but an hour
Hath intervened, of strange and fearful test?
Shouldst thou expect exemption? Then thy part

Were but a mean one; none should ever know
If gold thou wert, or only sparkling clay.
But trodden and defiled by feet of men,
Soon wouldst thou be forgotten. Yet thy place
Is on the very forehead of the world.

AMERICA.

This also would I know, for scorn hath met
Such weakness in me, that I live in doubt
Of any virtue — since my children hate
In part — I see not cause for any love.
And guilt in some discovered makes me fear
Lest such corruption, springing from the heart,
Have tainted all the members.

ANGEL.

    Yet not so,
For truth lifts high her sceptre in the land,
And loyalty is waxed to such a pitch
As earth hath never witnessed. Also prayers

AMERICA.

Ascend for thee, from lips that God regards,
Making the morning vocal, and the night,
And through the noisy noon they find a way
To heaven's gates; nor shall they plead in vain.

AMERICA.

Into a prayer, my heart that promise turns.

ANGEL.

Millions of hearts still brood and think on thee,
Of thee is all their counsel. Fear not thou,
Though some do temper still their faithful love
With meek submission, waiting for His will,
Who rules the nations, since therefrom no loss
Unto thy cause shall come. Hear even now
How one discourses with her secret soul.

VOICE OF A WOMAN VERY FAR AWAY.

Out of the South the battle-fiend up-soars;
He shakes a banner, red with brother's blood,

And from the utmost borders comes a cry
Answering the baleful signal. Wildly leaps
The nation's heart of fire. To arms they throng,
And o'er the advancing myriads, lightning-robed,
Hovers the avenger. O my land, my land!
Thine hour is on thee. God has lifted high
His sword, long sheathed — now shall be known
    through thee
Justice exalted over all vain schemes
Of little souls, mad with self-worshipping;
Now truth shall speak in accents to be heard
By those who can not hear the inward voice
Or words prophetic, out of lips of love.
Be not thou deaf upon this chosen day,
So shall its hours be shortened, and no stroke
Too deeply smite; — thy vigor shall return,
Thy course proceed with joy, thou yet shalt taste
Jehovah's bounties without measure poured
O'er the obedient land that seeks his name.
Yet know I not what destinies o'erhang

AMERICA.

The coming years,—with mournful heart I wait
And watch the gathering omens. These no joy,
No promise bring; no hour is this for pride,
Light boasts, and careless triumph. Now behoves
On sin to think, and with abased mien
Implore compassion, lest our load of guilt
Amid these waves should sink us utterly.
Yet unto one who still with earnest eyes
Follows and marks the goings forth of Him
Who rules amid the thunders, Hope is born
Daughter of Faith, with meek Experience joined.
Nor will he fear, knowing that thus of old
Evil is made the minister of good,
And that the headlong will of selfish man
Still works the purpose of a calmer choice,
Serene in wisdom. So I look on thee,
My country, and the love I bear thy soil
Grows the fair sequel of a higher far,
Wherewith in patriot links my heart is joined
Unto my truer birthland; her in thee

I ever see, and for her sake thy peace
Is dear, and though when gayly on the breeze
Thy colors float, the blood within my veins
Dances for exultation and for joy,
Yet with a deeper thrill I see in thought
Above the heights of that celestial home,
A blood red banner float in air serene,
Our tumults reach not, nor shall any hand
Of foe or rebel shake it where it stands,
Guarded with power eternal. Round it throng
The hosts of God's redeemed, name after name
Answering the roll-call. Gladly go they forth
To spread the peaceful triumphs of their King.
This is my land beloved, whose fairer shore
I see afar in visions of the night;
And when I wake, her thought is with me still.

AMERICA.

This is a sacred mood, and yet methinks
It waked a chord within me. We are dull,

We spirits of the nations — slow to read
The great decrees of God.

ANGEL.

Yet if thou hear,
There comes a strain on ruder voices borne,
Of more terrestrial import. Hear what songs
O' nights thy warriors sing, who lift their hearts,
Counting thy praises o'er in measures wild,
That yet through harmony of loving truth
Claim in thine ear a welcome. List! they come.

VOICES OF SOLDIERS SINGING.

First Chorus.

Who will thy glory sing,
  Land fair and wide?
Who make thy name to ring
  Loud, in his pride?

Sure never land like thee
    Meriteth song,
Sweet soil of liberty,
    God bless thee long.

How the sad age of men
    Painfully crept!
Thee, in his mighty arms,
    Ocean still kept.

Still, save of soulless things,
    Cattle, or bird
Through the wild wood that sings,
    Voice was not heard.

Save the wild hunter tribe,
    Feeble and few,
Thee, and thy gifts in store,
    No man yet knew.

Then, in his faithfulness,
    God, o'er the sea,
Guided the stately ships
    Even to thee.

Second Chorus.

Wide was the portal thrown,
    Swiftly they came,
Left the close prison-house,
    Bondage and shame.

Sick of old tyrannies,
    Forms that were dead,
Life that in fetters lay,
    Hither they fled.

Then, from the people's heart
    Went a new cry,
"Liberty! Liberty!"
    Win her, or die.

AMERICA.

Out of thy coast, my land,
  Went forth the voice,
How did the fettered ones
  Shout and rejoice!

Here on thy soil, my land,
  Stood, face to face,
Slavery, Liberty,
  Each for the race.

Here on thy soil, so dear,
  Once and for all
Was the great battle set:
  How shall it fall?

First Chorus.

Made ye not answer loud,
  Fathers renowned?
Answer — that tyrant-hearts
  Quailed at the sound?

Answer—when lifting
  In liberty's name,
Our star-lighted banner
  Ye fought for the same?

Always in glory bright
  Nobly maintained?
Unto your true-born sons
  Handed unstained!

All.

Lo! for the battle-rage
  Still waxes high,
Liberty! Slavery!
  One is the cry.

Still the one battle-field
  Where it began,
Still the same banner bright
  Floats in the van.

Still the wide world looks on,
  Knowing before,
Freedom, here falling,
  Falls evermore.

Shout, O America!
  Shout, unto these.
Shout, O great mountains!
  Lakes that are seas.

Shout, O ye mighty shores
  By either flood!
Shout! ye brave hearts of men
  Rich with true blood.

Shout! that not utterly
  Freedom shall fail,
God hath uplifted her,
  Bids her prevail.

AMERICA.

Who stands to live for her,
   Who stands to die,
Hark! from thy valleys deep
   Millions reply.

There bleed the noble sons
   Where the sires bled.
Land, thy true-hearted ones
   All are not dead.

Still art thou glorious,
   Land fair and wide,
Worthy our joyous hope,
   Worthy our pride.

Still we shall shout from thee,
   Loud o'er the sea,
Hither, ye captive ones,
   Haste, and be free.

AMERICA: (*after a pause.*)

They pass and leave night silent, but their song
A happier thought hath wakened. That new mood,
Born of my trouble, seems awhile to yield.

ANGEL.

Forget thy sorrow. Think as thou wast wont,
Take up thy courage. Think with these brave souls
On what thou wast, and art, and yet mayst be.

AMERICA.

In no mean place the Lord of heaven and earth
Hath set me, and I know that deed of his
Assures me safety, if I hold his word.

ANGEL.

Not for thyself thou art, but he through thee
Poured favors out on man. So if thou fall,
On man, and not on thee, shall rest the loss.

AMERICA.

AMERICA.

Angel, I know that man is dear to God,
And that since earth began, his love outruns
The nimble-footed sin with swifter stride.

ANGEL.

Though evil seem to conquer, yet that show
Shall vanish, and the conquered rise to snatch
A laurel from the bosom of defeat.
Stay up, stay up thy heart!

The SPIRIT OF REBELLION *appears.*

AMERICA.

     Ha! ha! what shape
Lowers at me from yon glen—my blood grows thick
With curdling horror. — Back! — avaunt, thou foe!
Still it advances, — and with threatening glare
Its looks assails me — all my spirit fails,

The storms that shook return with wilder rage;
I faint, — I perish.

ANGEL.

Still I hold thy hand.

SPIRIT OF REBELLION.

Now is my work accomplished, I can choose
Some summit of these hills, and without need
Of further motion, watch the play proceed
To consummation; as in prosperous years
When rain, dews, winds, sun, and heat-shrouding
    clouds
Are in the farmer's counsel. He but waits,
His seed once planted, till the germs mature,
And the rich autumn bring, without his toil,
The spoil forecounted. — Nay, I even take
First fruits of triumph, as in many ways,
So also now, proud tyrant, seeing thee
Stand there with threatening looks, so impotent.

AMERICA.

Haughty thou wast, and boastful from the first,
And as I note thee, still. I like it well.
No less contempt shall wait upon thy fall,
Or scorn surround the mention of thy name
Forever after; when I've proved to men
Of what vain wind, and worse than empty breath
Thy promises were made. I like to think
How soon my foot, that once could not be bold
To cross thy threshold, scarce the pains will take
To push thee from the path by which I walk
To perfect empire. — Is the lightning left
That scorched me once or twice some time ago,
Leaping from eyes so vengeful? I am healed
And stronger for the seasoning, and have proved
The quality of those fires. Lo! here I stand
Prevalent, of their fury unafraid,
Already master of a subtler force,
Deadlier to those I hate, as well thou knowest,
Writhing even now beneath it, though so still
In awe-affecting calmness thou canst stand

As words disdaining. Yet I know thy tongue
Hath not lost power of speech, that hath betrayed
Thy weakness to these winds, now muttering out
Through every cave and hollow of the hills
Defeat and fear and grinding agony,
Proving thy soul more abject than the slave,
Blindfold beneath the thick descending lash.
Still proud, still silent? But a step or two
I take, and smite that circlet from thy brow
That marks thee still as sovereign.

Spirit of Union *appears, and speaks.*

Back, accursed!
Stand back, till first thy fell and impious hand
Accomplish my destruction: then, with mine
That sacred life shall own a tie so close
There needs no blow directer. Both thine aims
End thus in one.

Rebellion.

Whence then hast thou appeared?

I struck thee, left thee prostrate, thought thee
    dead:
For not my steel I trusted, nor my strength,
Knowing thee vigorous, — but with careful skill
And slow invention, such a poison mixed
As, entering thy fair body with the wound,
Fouled all the taintless blood. I smile to see
The marks of such disturbance, in black lines
Written so thick all over that soft skin,
Once spotless in its brightness, — in quick breaths,
Twitchings of restless features, as if pain
Pulled at the strings of life, and in thy limbs
Some strange distortions, such as were not wont
To mar their godlike grace. I gather hope,
Seeing at least, if not the very self,
The ante-signs of death.

UNION.

                True is thy word,
Yet not all true, O boaster! Even thou—

Nay! none so well — hast known that art nor
    spell,
Could mix a drug so potent, but this frame,
If strong in native health, should cast it out
As fountains what defiles them, or else change
And make subservient. So thy purposed work
Was longer and more secret. Ere I knew,
Strange languor unexplained, importing ill,
Had taken half the vigor from these limbs,
And dull and creeping symptoms of disease,
More fatal, as less noticed, paved the way
For death to enter, when thy bolder hand
Should thrust him on me, at some chosen hour.
Such was thy plan; but if the end shall prove
The crafty venom, and the open sword,
Both impotent alike, and greater strength
Born of the greater contest, and the proof
Of native force unguessed, until the act
Of agony that tested, then to me
Pure gain accrues, and this not last nor least,

AMERICA.

I know my foe, I know him and his might,
And all his ways of cunning, and shall meet
Henceforth as one so armed. — Nay, I believe
Already thou hast felt thy blows recoil,
Which, if it should imply, though felt at first
But slightly, some such vast and hideous ill
As that fell stroke intended, aimed at me,
If failure meant defeat, and not to slay,
Thyself to lie at last among the slain,
Perchance thou now canst guess. What! dost
    thou start?
Some eloquence within, that met my words,
Filled out my meaning there, and caused thee
    make
That gesture of despair.

REBELLION.

                Such speech is cheap;
I skirmish not with breath. A twinge that came
And passed before 'twas felt, means something else

I fancy, than thy sounding threats portend.
Failure?—Ha! Ha!—Defeat?—I take thy sense
To be some other than old custom sets
To such articulations. But, for thee,
What madness holds thee? What hast thou to do
To save this crazy state? I with main strength
Have snapped thy weakened cords, felt long ago
As fetters, lately proved more dissoluble
Than once thy boastings gave us leave to see.
What's left to thee, self-stripped—by flattering talk
Of freedom, loyalty enforced by love,
Willing submission to an equal yoke,
Felt so as none—of power that might have dwelt
In bonds coercive? That vile cant o'erthrown,
I scarce have need to measure words with thee.

UNION.

Fiend! whose foul plots, and now more open war,
Have marred so far the fair tranquillity
That like an atmosphere had wrapped about

AMERICA.

This country of my choice, — know that not vain
The slow advance of ages, not in vain
That noble state now stands, whose living sap
Is union. This, both power and law, shall prove;
Obeyed in joyous freedom, while men know
Their highest glory, but, this wisdom lost,
Still are they used, not using. Still goes on
The mighty deed of life. They cannot choke
The ample channels, but the genial tide
Finds soon a way, sweeps them along its course,
Flows on triumphant. Still my glorious tree
Uprears its giant branches to the sun,
Brother of clouds and dew, and gathering strength
From storms alike and sunshine, — from soft airs
Sighing among its summer-painted boughs,
And frosts, whose slender needles prick among
Its tender roots in winter. Still returns
The season of its fruitage, food and joy
Remain, and shelter good for all who come.

REBELLION.

Deal thou in breath. For me, I'll cut thy tree,
Ay! hew it at the roots, and turn it up
To whiten in the sun. What! canst not see
(I know not why I wait and talk with thee)
In what a hell of ruin thou art plunged,
Thou, and thy favorites with thee? Look about,
Come up to yonder height. We can from thence
Behold our arguments, all spread about
In forms of ready logic. Lo! what sight
Confutes thee ere thou speak. The world can see
What love thy nurslings, dandled on thy knees,
Bear thee — grown old enough to understand
What fools thy flatteries made them. And for those
Who stand as in thy name, to trample down
The natural rights and lawful liberties
Of their so cherished brethren, why, 'tis plain
Against thy will they do't, and o'er thy neck
Rush on that foul injustice. I am glad

AMERICA.

They did not tamely yield. Their act refutes
Their reason for it, and thee and them involves
In such a paradox as endless time
Shall never reconcile. I'll leave thee then
To deal with that. My part to glory now
In full success, that long ago o'erpassed
The boundaries of my hope, and swells each day
Into a very ocean, flooding wide
Thy old dominion, soon by strictest search
To be discerned no more.

    SPIRIT OF SLAVERY *appears.*

      What ho! good friend.
Welcome, old comrade, yet what storms of wrath
Brew in thine eyes, and seem on me to fall?

    SPIRIT OF SLAVERY.

O boaster! without me, what hope hadst thou
To stir this mighty fabric, now o'erthrown,
Because I, I was in it from the first

Laid in among the mortar and the stones
That seemed its firm foundation, — deeper yet
A fatal quicksand, underneath it hid,
And as its solid walls securely rose,
Pinned in, among the rest, a timber fair
To outward sight, but inwardly corrupt
And crumbling to the hammer. This being so,
How could it else but fall? I grudge thee much
Thy self-exalting—but am thus content,
When the last crash shall come, that scarce had
 come
So soon, but for thy meddling, as I own,
But little shall be left for thee, or me,
Or any, nay, I know not who shall gain.
I lose my great security, but thou
Mayst go to sleep forever, since thy deed
Shall safely thrive, nor any end be found
Of that rank harvest; as an evil seed
Will spread, and spread, till none can root it out,
But all the land is poisoned.

AMERICA.

REBELLION.

What care I?
My end is gained.—And boast not thou so loud,
As sole efficient of my finished deed,
Though thou alone wert ruin. Other beams
Wormed through, I know, and rotten to the heart,
Built into this fair house, though painted o'er
So well that none save I, whose eyes have searched
Each undiscovered flaw, had found it out.
Nay, I could make confession larger still,
Sweep all in one, and say, that sin itself,
All weakening, all corrupting, both in thee
Working, and elsewhere, — under social forms,
Uses of commerce, policies of states,
Castes, customs, private lusts, and public wrong,
Sin is my guaranty, excites my hope,
Finds me a foothold, puts his hand with mine
And crowns me when I triumph! O'er this land
I look, and see it drowned and choked with sin;
Toward God I look, remembering that his throne

Endured not sin of old, and this old scar
Of his once headlong vengeance stirs me up.
I call on him to help me,—rather use
My arm, to bring his ready thunders down
On these offenders. Such a prayer I think,
E'en from my lips well suits him, whom I know
A God of justice.

     AMERICA.

       Is there none to help,
Am I then given up an ungrudged prey
For hell to feed on, while the heavens look down
From their high place approving? Was it this,
This so near bourne, and limit set to all,
That from fate's niggard hand, without my prayer,
Tempted so lavish bounties? Summers short
Are plenteous, but my fruits are yet to taste,
My vines ungathered, nay! the cruel snows
Cut off the very flowers that from their stalks
Nodded in sweet assurance of the time,
So far from winter's threshold. Ah! too soon

Mine hour has found me, and the hounds of death
Smell out my hidden crimes, to tear them down,
Me with them also, me and all whose life
Had centred at my heart. Shall it be thus?
O God! shall sin prevail? — shall former grace
Count nothing? Is there nothing in me left
To claim thy pity even? — no faith, no truth?
No loyalty, no wide beneficence,
Without the hope of guerdon exercised?
No spark of any virtue, that should shield
A little from these storms? — yet should I plead
The things my soul remembers? doubtless all
Stand uneffaced forever in his book.
He knows, and yet his judgments fall like hail,
And I lie bruised beneath, and can not rise.

Voice of Earth *is heard from below.*

EARTH.

Cease now, my daughter, cease this vain lament,
For what to thee hath happened, save the lot

Common to nations ? From mine ancient seat,
Since God appointed man to tread my face,
Mine eye hath marked his goings, and discerned
Of all his plans and hopes, his marvelous schemes
And high achievement, one sole end assured,
When for himself and them he seeks at last
Some chamber of my always open grave.
All over my broad surface, East and West,
Lie strewed the wrecks of empires, that his hand
Once raised to glory, — but no base so strong
His hand contrived for any, that some wind
Of adverse fortune brought not down at last
Its towering pride, and made it lie as low
As each that went before it. All alike
Proclaim in long succession how his work
Is error, all, and failure. If he hits
Some hidden wisdom in his random path,
Still he o'erlooks, or, seeing, underrates,
Or, rightly understanding, yet prefers
The present pleasure to the greater good,

Or choosing well, yet through unsteadfast will
Lets slip erelong the treasure half secured,
And with the crowd goes headlong. This last
    proof
Should not for aye be lacking, and thy name
Must to thy mighty list of perished states
Add yet its fading lustre. Why shouldst mourn
If as thy fame was greater, so thy fall
Comes sooner? Not to heaven impute the cause,
Nor on thyself too heavy burden lay
Of rash remorseful censure. Since with man's
Thy destiny is one, thy wisdom still
Swayed by the rule of his, and as he is
Thou art in all things, while of him I know
No virtue constant, but his every deed,
Like that same dust of which his God him made,
Owns fealty to winds, and changing tides,
Rather than any law by truth prescribed,
Or reason in him planted. So my soul
Yearns o'er him still, seeing him always own

His ancient kinship, and so well betray
What unto me belongs of all he is,
Though lifted high among the meaner tribes
Of my less gifted offspring. Well I know
The source of his decay, nor greatly chide
That frailty, by whose sure effect at last
He lays his head down, whence he reared it first,
And mingles with my clods his glorious frame.

 Thou also be content, I counsel thee,
Take now thy portion as it falls, and share
The fortunes of thy lord. For thou shalt lose
With life, no good that should not cost thee dear
Beyond its proper worth, through cares and toils,
Anxieties and fears. But shorter fate
Implies thy sorrows shorter, and thy doom
Less terrible, than if through longer course
Of years, prepared, and fruit of many crimes.

AMERICA.

Are these the voices that pronounce my doom?

AMERICA.

Earth! thou hast spoken. Now let Heaven unfold
Her portents, then will I believe.

REBELLION.

Look up,
Behold the sign! — O thou accursed light!
Mine eyes are blinded.

ANGEL OF VENGEANCE *descends with a flaming scroll, open in his hand. Speaks.*

Over this foul land
I hang the doom that God's just wrath awards
Unto its many crimes. A little while
The cloud of indignation shall uphold
Its black tempestuous burden — e'er it rend
The covering of the heavens, and be poured out
In one wide wasting ruin. Let men read
The condemnation, manifest to all.
The doom of such a land as lifting high
The cry of justice, liberty for all,

Hath still approved, and cradled at her side
The worst of wrong, the tyranny whose shame
Gives every other leave to lift again
Its head, once bowed before her arrant boasts,
And at her text's brave comment sneer and laugh,
A land that makes of freedom and of right
Excuse for every sin, whereby man mocks
His God, and harms his brother, and pollutes
The very founts of blessing, turning all
To poison and a curse. For such a land
Behold God's sentence. From the sin shall come
The ruin more direct than arrow flies
From bended bow, or from the widening breach
The wall's destruction. So that all shall know
What caused this utter fall, and see therein
And praise the perfect justice of our God.

AMERICA.

Pity! O Lord! Thus groveling on my face,
Thus without plea, excuse, or any hope,

AMERICA.

Save in the one Name thou hast taught to man,
I still remember, though the pains of death
Take hold upon my soul, that thou art Love.

The ANGEL OF MERCY *descends.*

SLAVERY.

I fall! I fall! blasted with utter light.

ANGEL OF MERCY.

Swift messenger of vengeance, I at last
O'ertake the meteor course that fell so swift,
Since first the word went forth, down the steep
      chasms
Of yawning night, to bear the signs of wrath;
But in my mouth another speech was put,
Another scroll than thine my hand enfolds,
Thine open is, mine sealed.—Thy message, clear,
Thy proclamation in all ears resounds,
But mine is secret still. Yet be it known,

Seeing that God hath sent me, there is hope—
Mercy still lives, and heaven forgets not man.

ANGEL OF COMFORT.

Lift up thy head, O stricken one! and drink
The balm that Heaven vouchsafes thee.

AMERICA.

      I thank God!
And yet my heart is dull, my brain confused,
I understand not any thing. I seem
A field once fair and fruitful, which the storms
Have beaten, and the water-floods made waste,
Which, though the rain hath ceased, lies prostrate
  still,
Mingling its riches with the muddy soil.

ANGEL.

Take comfort.

AMERICA.

    Is there pardon then, in truth?

AMERICA.

Shall I yet flourish as in days of old?
Oh! that I heard the voice of destiny,
My soul should listen, while the great decree
Fell from his lips that can not speak but right.

The ANGEL OF DESTINY *descends.*

ANGEL OF DESTINY.

O Spirit of a nation! whose high state
And happy lot hangs now to view of men
Balanced upon the edge and turning-point
Of some most fearful change, which, once com-
    plete,
Implies to man great loss, but to his foes
New and most signal triumph. I am come
At hearing of thy voice, and to thy prayer
Such answer bring as leaves inviolate still
The things ordained as secret, till their time
Brings their unfolding. Unto Him that rules
Leave also perfect knowledge. But take thou,

Freely vouchsafed, such light whose honest use
Shall make thee wise enough for all thy need.
No new disclosure from the pitying skies
I bring, but things thine ears have often heard
Unheeding, things once known, but, in this strait,
Not present as they should be to thy thought,
Though nearest to thy need. For much men cry,
Straining their eyes towards heaven, as hoping thence
Some special gift to tumble from the blue,
While all they lack lies waiting at their feet,
And trips them ere they heed it. Ready lies,
Provided long ago, the utmost good
Unto man's want proportioned: but his looks
Turn not that way, and thou, allied to him,
By equal error blinded, now must learn
Thy youth's first lessons o'er, which, though they sound
Simple, are worthy yet an angel's tongue.
 Know first, or first remember, to what end

AMERICA.

Nations arise or perish. Hast thou heard
Of these each several record, what began
Their upward courses, what to each belonged
Of greatness, how they served, and how betrayed
Each cause sublime committed to their trust?
How of their worth, continuance, of their crime
Decay ensued and fall? One work for all,
Varied in each by nature's several bent,
Eternal love intended — but alike
All turned aside, and to some private lust
Debauched their glory. Love, not turned so soon
From that fair plan, made even wills averse
Serve unaware and minister some good
To bless the ages, though themselves were left
To take their own poor choice, and lose at last
Even that part of good, whose scanty charms
Enticed them from the whole, and so their fall
Came close upon their grandeur's utmost height.
Their service done, some new estate of power
Swallowing the past, — itself foredoomed to know

Like limits in the future — these in most
Adjusted by some happy natural gift,
Tact, genius, power to rule, or warlike might,
Or skill in commerce, yet in all alike
Proportioned to one plan — whose exigence
Shortened their time of empire, or drew out
To length, by no internal worth explained.

AMERICA.

Too well I knew, too well, the common doom,
And how comes back the thriftless prodigal
A beggar to the gates. I counted not,
But lavished out my portion. It is just.

ANGEL OF DESTINY.

Yet think more deeply if thou wouldst be wise,
And know that fruitful root whence trouble
    springs.

AMERICA.

Speak—that I may be wise, in hearing thee.

AMERICA.

ANGEL OF DESTINY.

States are ordained for man, — he in himself
Being that proper state, whose government
Employs the eternal counsels. There behold
The first disorder, anarchy and schism,
Which from the one the many doth infect,
And breeds the public ills. He, since he fell,
No longer stands in archetypal grace
The perfect pattern after which should rise,
Fair in proportion, strong in unity,
The social fabric. Rather in him reigns
Confusion, all his faculties at war,
The noblest put the last, the mean ones first,
These trampling those, and those through slavish
    fear,
Or cramped and dulled with suffering, yielding
    still
Compliance undue, implying all alike
Debased and miserable. Seest thou well
What evils vex the nations? Should the sea

Be sweeter than its waves, or wilt thou make
Out of much dust, one pearl?

     AMERICA.

      Though I aspired,
I aimed beneath perfection.

    ANGEL OF DESTINY.

      Yet below
That mark, what safety?

     AMERICA.

      Angel! I am bold
As one who pleads for life. States are as man,
So hast thou taught me,—vexed and overthrown,
Because, through disobedience, he hath lost
The harmony within. Yet unto man
Hath God vouchsafed no hope? Why then
  goes on
This agony? Why rather doth not heaven

Shut down at once the awful night of doom
And make an end forever?

ANGEL OF DESTINY.

     Yet if God
More gloriously had wrought, — some brighter
 thing
Had caused to spring amid this wreck of time?

AMERICA.

I praise him! — for he dealeth wondrously.

ANGEL OF DESTINY.

For he hath bought redemption, at what price
Archangels dared not utter, till his deed
Taught their rapt ears another name for love,
By whose effect the man, a higher strength
Receiving, set in tune with perfect law
In all the powers he owns, need never fear
A second time to lose his happy lot,

Assured by mighty tokens, both from God
And manifest within. Seest thou that state,
Through all whose members perfectly had wrought
Such marvelous healing? Seest thou what life
Were hers, what fearlessness, what sure defense
Against all foes without? Of foes within
What confidence, and how her wealth's increase,
Her wisdom, power, and gladness had no bound?
Though such an one on earth hath never been,
Nor yet one perfect man (save HE that joined
To man's the strength divine) hath walked unstained
Her paths polluted, yet the grace of heaven
Makes earth a place to work in, here prepares
Parts of a pure and precious harmony,
Whose full accord shall all at once swell out
Upon His chosen day — and thrill afar
The angels in their music-bearing spheres.
Out of these ruins, scattered far and wide,
Betokening only loss, shall God upbuild

A city of his own, a state composed,
Not after dead and outward rules of law,
But by the vital energy of love:
A growth, complete as any fairest flower
That brightens in the sun, or vine that tempts
With plenty sweet the thirsty passers by.
But thou, O scarce believing! scarce aware
What words like these portend, lift up thine eyes,
And tell me what report they bring thee home.

AMERICA.

Angel! the vision is of other days,
New things I see and men, a realm of peace
Transfigured with pure light, whose sacred touch
Makes beauty where it rests. How my dull
    thoughts
Slink back ashamed, while I behold indeed
My fairest dream's fulfillment, but set high
Above its utmost daring. See what grace,
What dignity, what glory decks the form

I know as man's! Angel! deceive me not,
Are these my children, mine that walk the streets,
The golden pavement of that city fair?
Familiar are their faces as the sun,
And now as glorious. Whither are they come?
And by what path? and how shall men aspire,
As rightly hoping such estate of bliss
May at the end receive them? And to me
What signifies this sight, which thou hast shown,
Intending me some comfort, and to lift
My soul above the loss this hour portends?

ANGEL OF DESTINY.

This is the kingdom, and the reign of God,
Whose deep foundations, long in secret laid,
Shall stand unshaken, when the shows of things
Called real have vanished. Then shall come to
    view
What underneath this gross external shell
Matured unseen its strength, and drunk in life

Where all in death seemed silent. Then shall
    shout
All creatures that are ministers to man,
Seeing at last their homage and their faith
Approved, and sealed as just, while he appears
All glorious, of the many works of God
Fairest and most divine. So also thou
Canst not be else than glad, knowing before,
That surely as the truth of heaven prevails,
Out of thy thorniest cares, thy woes and pains,
This flower shall blossom, and its odorous heart
Be opened to the skies. Hence, first of all
Take comfort, and as this can give support,
Measure the hope that yet some wished for task
Awaits thy willing hand,—not yet expired—
For One whose love can estimate aright
Her office and its end—the proper term
Of happy service. By this law is sealed
The destinies of nations, first, as each
Bears on its earthly face some likeness fair

Of that celestial pattern, shows to men
Some shadow of that grace, and by such laws
Is governed, as in that pure liberty
Work out the life of love,—to gifts so fair
Continuance shall not fail, He that bestows
Such wisdom, shall not lightly make it vain.
Yet on a safer hope thy heart may rest,
Since 'tis the perfect state that God regards,
Making all histories and acts of time
That way to work, that meaning to write out
Letter by letter, till he finish all.
Thou, working with him too, with willing heart
Lending thine aid, not blindly, but that light
Well used—so freely poured, that many err
Slighting the common gift,—so shalt insure
Triumph in every conflict—unashamed
Meet all the fierce assaults of earth and time.
Nay! could this be, could any state on earth,
So armed with constant wisdom, turn her eyes
From shows of power, to truth's enduring crown,

Then might she hope one day, without much loss
Even of that she seemed, to drop aside
With her loved pupil, man, this dress of clay,
And mount, complete in robes of victory,
The welcome-giving skies.

AMERICA.

    Well do I know
This can not be for me, yet through thy word
My heart revives. I see a hope, at last
Strong confidence upholds me, that my cause
Wars not with truth, and that her foes are mine.
Therefore, O angel! while my many sins
Oppress me, and the follies of my sons,
So that, with these weighed down, I scarce can lift
My forehead from the dust, I yet recall
Teachings not wholly slighted, light vouchsafed
In some peculiar measure, not unused,
And mercies shown in timely chastisements.

Whereof I think my thoughts, in after days
Taking account, shall reckon as not least
Measured by previous sin, or present pain,
Or after fruit of good, this that now turns
My sweets to bitter.—Of these things I take
Some balm of glad assurance, well can trust
That pitying guidance still, that led my feet
Into this wilderness, apart from men,
And showed me things that others had not known,
And new and separate mercies,—knowing well
How I should use them, knowing too, I trust,
How by his faithful providence, my ways
Should ever be amended, till their course
Went clear and straight to right and happy ends.
Not in this flush and promise of my morn
Doth he intend such ruin, not so soon
That I, with all the fresh and untried gifts
He, for the sake of man, bestowed on me,
Should o'er the brink of such destruction fall.
So never more, I fear, to human wish

AMERICA.

Such promise would return, but all in vain
His heart go mourning through the coming days
The irretrievable and perfect loss.

ANGEL OF DESTINY.

Well dost thou argue from man's threatening loss
Some token that the love which follows man
Will for his sake deliver,—well dost trace
The future's promise, written in the past,
Since of one piece is all that work divine
Done on the face of earth, and if thy heart
Tell thee, and conscience whisper in her seat
That, howsoever thou hast gone astray,
Yet, thou hast prized God's favors, canst recall
Some use he must approve, some acts of love,
And liberal deeds of world-wide charity,
Some help accorded from thy happy seat
To those who strove with famine, or the hand
Of ready welcome reaching out to meet
The fugitive and wanderer in their need;

If with such memories thou canst prop thy heart,
Glad be thy courage then, though not to rest
Even here too surely—since thy best of deeds
Paid not thy debt, and if that heavenly love
Has some great good thy blind eyes could not
    see
Wrapped in this present ruin, not for thee
The plea of well desert, and blessings used
In full and glad obedience. Rather this
Should be thy stay, whatever thee befall,
The vision shall not fail,—thy youth's pure dream
Shall yet prove real—thou hast not been in vain.

AMERICA.

Strange comforts, angel, dost to me propose;
But thou, I think, to some sublimer sphere
Dost lift my thoughts, companioned with thine
    own.
Well!—if the mood might last. Yet who that
    once

AMERICA.

Unto the power of truth hath yielded up
His soul within him, ever quite shall lose
The memory of that sweetness? So to mine
This moment's revelation shall be gain
Whatever come behind, and for all war
My spirit with new strength be fortified.

ANGEL OF DESTINY.

Yet farther counsel. If the will of Heaven
Intend thee now deliverance, and once more
Thou at the head of nations stand, in hope
And joyful promise; thus henceforth be wise
By aims that follow God's,—by justice shown
In public deeds, by liberal works of love,
By virtue cherished, and the fear of God
In hearts of all thy children,—by good laws
Matured in thoughtful wisdom, thrusting out
With sharp or gentle force the evil code,
Oppression's hateful remnant,—by all acts
That lift the state, and give it surer hold

On God's great mercy manifest to man,
Unto thyself secure a longer course
Of prosperous wealth, and to thy happy sons
A heritage secure, which, used aright,
Shall be the pledge of nobler good to come,
Beyond the region and the reach of storms
That rage amid the shows and forms of time.

AMERICA.

Angel! I listen, and thy words are good.

ANGEL OF DESTINY.

See! earliest rays of morn begin to light
Faint signals in the East. For thee begins
A day of doubtful conflict. Yet be strong,
Be valiant, lend thy soul no more to fears,
But use thy hopeful courage, all shall be
As God disposes, and shall so be well.

FINIS.

www.ingramcontent.com/pod-product-compliance
Lightning Source LLC
Chambersburg PA
CBHW020143170426
43199CB00010B/872